Also by Evelyn McFarlane & James Saywell
If . . . (Questions for the Game of Life)

$If^2 \ldots$

If^2... $\bullet$ $\bullet$ $\bullet$

(500 New Questions for the Game of Life)

Evelyn McFarlane & James Saywell
Illustrations by James Saywell

Villard/New York

Library of Congress Cataloguing-in-Publication Data
McFarlane, Evelyn.
    If² . . . (500 new questions for the game of life)/ Evelyn McFar-
lane & James Saywell.—1st ed.
        p.   cm.
    ISBN 0-679-45286-9
        1. Conduct of life.   I. Saywell, James.   II. Title.
    BJ1581.2.M245   1996
170—dc20   96-19650

First Edition

If^2 . . .

The human imagination is infinite. The fantasies it creates thrill us and uplift us. They even help us to find our way in life. This second collection of "If . . ." questions picks up where its predecessor left off . . . somewhere deep in the extraordinary territory of what people hope for, dream for, and value about each other and themselves.

There is one immediate purpose of these 500 queries: to provoke the mind. Some are humorous, some more serious, and some even quite difficult to answer. Once you begin to play, you may find laughter, tears, revelation, learning, surprise, or contemplation. But you will never lack the potential for fascinating discussions.

As well as the "classic" topics (sex, money, children, death), If^2 . . . includes queries related to issues on the minds of people today, such as welfare, taxes, health care, the environment, and many more. Each of these alone can give rise to further discussion and other questions. Use this book to find out more about your neighbors or your friends; ask "If" questions of your teachers, use them for interviews, call in one to a radio show, send one out on the Internet. Few people can resist engaging in the discussions that "If . . ." initiates. The difficulty with thinking up and compiling these questions was that we were repeatedly interrupted by the irresistible urge to try to answer them, our own imaginations tempting us constantly from the asking, toward the answering. May you, too, give in completely to the same wonderful temptation.

If you found out for certain there is a Heaven and a Hell, how would you change your life?

If you could determine the age at which you will die, but with no guarantees regarding health or money, how old would you like to be when you go?

If you had to select the one thing in life you feel the most guilty about, what would it be?

If you could rid the earth of one thing, what would it be?

If you were to close down any charity, which one would you pick?

If you could have overheard a specific conversation between any two people, which would it be?

If you could have the hair of any Hollywood celebrity, whose would you want?

If you had to describe the most memorable night of your life, what would you say?

If you could have the power to hypnotize anyone for a day, who would you pick and what would you have them do?

If you had to name the best album cover ever, which would it be?

If you had to choose the one thing that gives you the most comfort, what would you say?

If you could have witnessed one event from your family's history, what would you want to see?

If you had to choose a single vice president in the history of the United States to become president, who would you pick?

If you had to give up your favorite food forever, what is the minimum amount of money you would demand in return?

If you had to name the best live musical performance you have ever attended, which would you pick?

If you had to name the best speech or presentation you've ever heard, what would it be?

If you had to name the one thing that most frightens you about growing old, what would it be?

If you could be more ambitious in only one aspect of your life, what would it be?

If you could have anyone from history welcome you into the afterlife, who would you want it to be?

If you had to nominate one person you have known for sainthood, who would you choose?

If you were to spend the rest of your life in the company of a single type of animal, which would you choose?

If you had to constantly carry a weapon of some kind, what would it be?

If you could trade your derrière for that of someone else, whose would you want?

If you had to name the one most important ingredient of human beauty, what would you say it is?

If you had to give a prize for the most sexually attractive politician in U.S. history, who would win it?

If you had to name the single most erotic part of the human body, what would it be?

If you had to name the least erotic part of the human body, what would it be?

If you were to add a thirteenth month to the year, where would you insert it?

11

If you could rid your family of one thing, what would it be?

If you had to name the all-time best song, which would you pick?

If you could say (or have said) one thing to your father on his deathbed, what would it be?

If you could have one thing made out of pure gold, what would you choose?

If you had to pick one experience or situation when you were the most decisive, which would it be?

If you could have only one part of your body massaged every day, what part would you choose?

If you could be the character in any spy novel, who would you choose to be?

If you had to name the time when you came closest to death, when would it have been?

13

If you could make anyone in the world do something each day, who would it be, and what would you have them do?

⊷ ⊨✦⊨ ⊶

If you could reverse a single policy of the pope, what would you change?

⊷ ⊨✦⊨ ⊶

If you were to choose the breed you would be if you were a dog, which type would best suit you?

⊷ ⊨✦⊨ ⊶

If you had to name the one thing that repeatedly makes you angriest, what would it be?

14

If you could organize a family reunion with all of your dead relatives, where would you hold it?

If you could change one thing about the building you work in, what would you alter?

If you were to decide the legal age for sexual consent, what age would it be?

If you were to prescribe a cure for grief, what would it entail?

If someone were trying to woo your lover away from you, what methods would bring them the most success?

⊷ ⊰♦⊱ ⊷

If you had to name the one thing you have witnessed in your life that best represents Goodness, what would you say?

⊷ ⊰♦⊱ ⊷

If you could have modeled in one of Calvin Klein's advertising campaigns for either underwear or fragrance, which ad would you like to have been in?

If you had to name the best music album ever recorded, which would you select?

If you had to name the one time in your life when you were the most angry, when was it?

If you were to be killed by an animal, what kind would you want it to be?

If you were to be tied naked in bed and have your lover melt an ice cube on a single part of your body, without touching you otherwise, where would you want them to melt it?

If you could change one thing about your face to make it more beautiful, what would you alter?

17

If you had to choose the one animal or insect species that is most beautiful, which would you pick?

If you could have any view in the world visible from your bed, what would it be?

If you had to name the most beautiful bed you have ever occupied, what would it be?

If you could exchange work space (e.g., office or cubicle), but not jobs, with someone you presently work with, whose spot would you take?

If you could have prevented any single fashion idea or trend from ever happening, which would you have stopped?

If you were to select a moment when you were convinced that an angel was watching over you, when would it have been?

If you could suddenly find out that one work of fiction was actually true, what book would you select?

If you were to have bells ring out loud automatically (for all to hear) every time you did a certain thing, what would it be?

If you could have a single button beside your bed that did one thing, what would you want it to do?

If you could have any single kind of appliance attached to your bed, what would it be?

If you were to have Shakespeare to dinner tonight and could invite one other person from history, who would you pick?

If you could have prevented one book from ever having been written, which book would it be?

If there were to be one person, among those whom you know, who could from now on read all your thoughts, who would you have it be?

If you had a spot somewhere on your body that, when touched by anyone else, instantly gave you an orgasm, where would you want it to be?

If you could have had one person in your life be less candid with you than they were (or are), who would it be?

If you could have had one person in your life be more candid with you than they were (or are), who would it be?

21

If you had to name a smell that always makes you nostalgic, what would it be?

If you could train a pet bird to do one thing for you and always return home again, what would it do?

——— ✠ ———

If you could have been Judge Lance Ito, what one thing would you have done differently?

——— ✠ ———

If, in order to save your life, someone you know had to donate their heart to you (without dying), whose heart would you want inside yourself?

If you could have heard the deathbed confession of one person from history, who would you pick?

If you were going to die in ten minutes and could confess only one thing in order to pass with peace of mind, what would you say?

If you could change places with any of your friends, who would you choose to be?

If you could ruin someone's reputation, whose would it be, and how would you do it?

If you could be the house cat or lap dog of any person on earth, whose would you choose to be?

If you could cause any single person to change their mind about one thing or on one topic, who would you pick, and how would you change their thinking?

If you could wake up tomorrow in your own bed, but in another place anywhere in the world inside or outside, where would you like it to be?

If your children could read only four books while growing up, which would you have them read?

If you could eliminate a single kind of danger (other than death) for your children, what would it be?

—⊶ ⋈✦⋈ ⊶—

If you were to pick a city whose character best represents your own personality, which would you choose?

—⊶ ⋈✦⋈ ⊶—

If you could prevent someone you know from overusing one word, who would it be, and what word would it be?

—⊶ ⋈✦⋈ ⊶—

If you could see the inside of any single athlete's locker, whose would it be?

If you could have X-ray vision on one person you work with, who would you want it to be?

—·—≡♦≡—·—

If you could be more candid with one person you know from now on, who would it be?

—·—≡♦≡—·—

If you could have taken better care of one thing in your life, what would it have been?

—·—≡♦≡—·—

If you could change one thing about the way you were disciplined as a child, what would you alter?

26

If you suddenly found the courage to do one thing you have always been afraid of doing, what would you want it to be?

If you had to describe your worst experience with blood, what would you say?

＋ ≍◈≍ ＋

If you were to be the sole confessor of one person on earth, without being able to ever betray their trust no matter what they told you, who would you want it to be?

＋ ≍◈≍ ＋

If you could choose any three songs to compile on a disc to wake up (slowly) to every morning, what would they be, and in what order?

If you could have witnessed the childhood of someone famous, whose would it be?

If you had to exchange wardrobes with someone you know, whose clothes would you want?

＋－ ≡◆≡ －＋

If you could have won a single thing you tried for in your lifetime but didn't win, what would it be?

＋－ ≡◆≡ －＋

If you had to name your greatest conquest in life thus far, what would it be?

If you could keep only one book you currently own, which would you choose?

If you could have a set of bed sheets made of anything in the world, what material would you choose?

If you could have known someone as a child that you now know, who would it be?

If you had to name the worst song to wake up to in the morning, what would it be?

If you could commission any living author to write a new book, who would you choose, and what would you have them write about?

If you could have had your mind changed on one issue or decision in your lifetime, what would it have been?

If you could have changed the mind of one person from history on one issue, who and what issue would you pick?

If someone you work with could have X-ray vision on you, who would you most hate it to be?

If you were to start an orphanage for children anywhere in the world, where would you want it to be?

If you had to choose the single most charming person you have ever met, who would win?

—————— ⊠◊⊠ ——————

If just one aspect of your life functioned perfectly forevermore, what would you pick?

—————— ⊠◊⊠ ——————

If you had to pay one dollar for every time you thought of sex in any form, how long would it be before you went bankrupt?

If you could change one thing about the American electoral system, what would it be?

If you could solve one world problem by pledging your own permanent celibacy, what would you do it for?

If you could eliminate one thing other people's children do, what would it be?

If you had to name the most dangerous thing you have ever done on purpose, what would it be?

If you came home to find your teenage son or daughter in bed with a postal delivery person, what would you say to them in one sentence?

If you were to be paid to write a new book on any subject you wished, what would it be about?

If you had to eat the cooking of one person you know personally for the rest of your life, whose would you want it to be?

If you were to have three new baby daughters, what would you name them?

If you could give hair back to any balding person you know, who would you pick?

If you found out that there is no afterlife in any sense, how would you change your life?

If you had to name the one thing that really makes your day, what would it be?

If you had to name the one thing that can most readily ruin your day, what would it be?

If you could change one thing about your country's history, what would you alter?

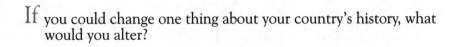

If you could change one nonphysical thing about your spouse or lover, what would it be?

If you had to eliminate one emotion from your life, which would it be?

If you could suddenly be irresistibly charming for one day only, what would you do?

If you could give a bronze cast of one part of your body to your most recent ex, what part would it be?

If you had to identify the one thing destiny probably held in store for you, what would you say it is?

If you could change one thing about your typical day, what would it be?

If you discovered a Shakespeare manuscript that no one else had ever seen, what would you do with it?

36

If you could be right behind any single person in line at the Gates of Heaven, who would you choose?

—————✦—————

If you found yourself at the Pearly Gates and had one chance to make your case for entry, what would you say?

—————✦—————

If you had to name your greatest accomplishment so far in life, what would you say it was?

If you could have back one article of clothing you gave or threw away, what would you want it to be?

If you were to name something that your parents or spouse should have felt guilty about but didn't, what would it be?

If you had to name the most gullible person you know, who is it?

If you could stop loving someone, who would it be?

If you suddenly found yourself at work, wearing women's erotic underwear and nothing else, what would you say (in one sentence) to your fellow workers?

If you could enact one law related to royal marriages, what would it say?

If you could give one thing to each of your ex-lovers, what would you give them?

——— ⊫✦⊨ ———

If you had to name the person who turned out to be furthest from your first impression of them, who would it be?

——— ⊫✦⊨ ———

If you were to name the most clear proof that evil exists in the world, what would you say?

If you could drink only one type of alcoholic drink for the rest of your life, what would you choose?

If you had to fight a duel tomorrow at dawn, and you could determine the type of weapons you both would use, what would they be?

＋ ≡◆≡ ＋

If you could have the vocabulary of any person you know, who would you pick?

＋ ≡◆≡ ＋

If you had to leave everything you own to your alma mater, but you could specify what it would be used for, what would you request?

If you were to name the best "I told you so" you ever got to deliver, what was it?

--- ✠ ---

If you were to pick the one thing that always makes you smile, what would it be?

--- ✠ ---

If you had to choose the celebrity you most resemble in personality, who would it be?

--- ✠ ---

If you were to have two new baby sons, what would you name them?

41

If you had to confess to the most evil thing you have ever done, what would it be?

———— ✦ ————

If you had to name one advantage daughters have over sons, what would you say it is?

———— ✦ ————

If you could cause something that happened in the history of the world to happen again in order to teach something to those in the present, what would you have re-happen?

———— ✦ ————

If you could change places with any celebrity in the world, but would have to remain that person forever, who would you be?

42

If you had to name the nicest thing that has ever happened to you completely by chance, what would it be?

If you were to confess to how many people you have honestly been in love with, what would you say?

If you wanted your death to have the maximum dramatic effect on people who knew you, how would you choose to die?

If you had to give the same gift to everyone you know next Christmas, what would it be?

If you could touch any single person in the world with only the tip of your index finger, who would you pick, and where would you touch them?

If you had to receive the same (affordable) gift, besides money, from everyone you know on your next birthday, what would you want?

If, in retrospect, you could have been nicer to one person in your life, who would it be?

If you could stop overusing one word in your vocabulary, which word would it be?

If you could ask one yes or no question about your own death and have the answer now, what would you ask?

If you could have done one good deed that you had the opportunity to do but didn't, what would it be?

If you had to name the smartest person you have ever met, who would it be?

If you could make one thing come true for one friend, what would it be, and for whom?

If you had to identify the time or moment in your life when you felt the most free, when was it?

If you had to name the one personality trait that you have tried the hardest to change in yourself, what would you say?

If you had to name the most gentle person you know, who would it be?

If you could go back for one minute to the Garden of Eden and give Adam advice, what would you say?

If you could control the lens of a satellite for one hour, so that you could watch any spot on earth, where would you point it?

If you had to name the saddest thing you've ever witnessed, what would it be?

If you could have said one thing to Harry Truman the day before he decided to drop the atomic bomb, what would you have said?

If you lost feeling everywhere but in one small spot, where would you want the spot to be?

47

If you had to name the thing that most limits your freedom, what would it be?

If you could free yourself from one burden in your life, what would it be?

If you had to name the single best deed a stranger has done for you in your lifetime, what would it be?

If you could get God to do one thing to prove His existence, what would you ask Him to do to convince you?

If you could give an Academy Award to the most underappreciated actor in the history of Hollywood, who would you award it to?

If you could have changed one thing about your mother's life, what would it be?

If you had to name the most difficult good-bye you've ever said, what would it be?

If you could have one free service in your home every day, what would you take?

If you had to describe the silliest thing people do in general, what would you say?

— ⚹ —

If you could guarantee one thing about your next trip, what would it be?

— ⚹ —

If you could completely remove someone's vocal cords for a year, whose would they be?

— ⚹ —

If you had to name the most incredible thing a friend has ever done for you, what would it be?

50

If you were given academic tenure to teach any course you wished at any university in the world, where would you want it to be, and in what subject?

If you had to be buried inside any existing tomb or grave, and the tomb's name would be changed to yours, whose would you want to take over?

—— ❊ ——

If you could go back and fight any military battle differently, what battle would you pick, and how would you fight it?

—— ❊ ——

If you had to name the one time when you truly went "beyond the call of duty," when would it be?

If you had to name the physical characteristic of your mate that most resembles their parents, what would it be?

If you could have any number of siblings, how many would you have, and of what gender?

If you had to name the best and worst diets you've ever tried, which would win and which would lose?

If you had to name the most beautiful spot on earth that you've ever seen, what would you choose?

If you had to name the single most important thing in your life, what would it be?

———— ⚔ ————

If you had to say what one thing in your life best represents your freedom, what would it be?

———— ⚔ ————

If you had to name the single most important duty of a parent, what would you say it is?

———— ⚔ ————

If you had to identify what made the best teacher you ever had the best, what would you say it was?

53

If you could gain or lose weight in any one part of your body, where would it be?

—————— ✦ ——————

If you could advise one couple you know to separate, who would it be?

If you could have prevented one thing from happening between a friend and yourself, what would it have been?

—————— ✦ ——————

If the pope promised he would do one thing you asked of him, what would you ask?

If you had to name the grossest thing you have ever put in your mouth, what would it be?

--- ✦ ---

If God were to whisper one thing in your ear, what would you like Him to say?

--- ✦ ---

If you could do one thing that you've never done with a spray can of Reddi Whip, besides eat it, what would you do and to whom?

--- ✦ ---

If you were to be asked the most difficult thing you can imagine by your best friend, what would it be?

If you could have asked Jesus Christ one thing just before the crucifixion, what would it have been?

—————— ❈❖❈ ——————

If you could repair a relationship with one former friend, who would it be with?

—————— ❈❖❈ ——————

If you had to predict which famous couple were going to separate next, who would you pick?

If you had to pick the worst driver you know, who would win?

If you asked the most difficult thing you can imagine of your lover, what would it be?

<hr>

If you had to name the craziest thing you ever did in your youth, what would it be?

<hr>

If you had to choose the most extreme example of sexual harassment you have suffered, what would it be?

<hr>

If you could trade in-laws with anyone you know, whose would you take?

If you were to pick an object to be worshipped by a new religion, what would it be?

If you could retract one thing you've ever said, what would you take back?

———❦———

If you could tell any current world leader one thing as president of the United States, what would it be, and to whom would you say it?

———❦———

If you could ask the greatest sacrifice imaginable of a friend, what would it be?

If you were to identify the most important quality in a friend, what would you say it is?

If you had to pick the biggest Freudian slip you've ever made, what would it be?

If you had to repeat the worst thing you've ever said to your mother, what was it?

If you could have had more time together with someone you know, who would you want it to be with?

59

If you could have the chance to see what has become of one childhood friend, who would you choose to find out about?

If you had to name the single physical characteristic about yourself that most resembles your mother or father, what would it be?

If you had to nominate the best-dressed person you know, who would win?

If you had to name the one thing you envy most about your mate, what would it be?

If you had to name the most violent scene in a movie you have ever seen, what would it be?

If you could have had one thing that one of your friends has, what would you pick, and from whom?

If you could personally see one natural phenomenon that you have never seen, what would it be?

If you had to name the one person your mate knows who makes you jealous, who would it be?

If very good friends were visiting your town, where would you take them to eat if money were no object?

If you had to name the one thing that most easily makes your mate feel guilty, what would it be?

If you could take revenge on another driver, who would it be, and for what incident?

If you had to select one movie sequel that was superior to the original, what would it be?

If you could select a role model for each of your kids, who would you pick?

If you could completely redecorate any room in your house at someone else's expense, what room would you choose?

If you could decide how many times a year you saw your own parents, how often would it be?

If you could determine how often you see your in-laws, how often would it be?

If health were not an issue, how many times a month would you exercise?

If you had to describe the worst experience you've had in an automobile, what would it be?

＋—— ✠ ——＋

If you had to name the most overrated actor in Hollywood, who would it be?

＋—— ✠ ——＋

If you could open and run any kind of restaurant anywhere, what kind of food would you serve, and where?

If you had to name the three most important family values in order of importance, what would they be?

If you could have decided the outcome of the O. J. Simpson trial, what would your verdict be?

If you could have any single Hollywood celebrity be your slave for a weekend, who would you pick?

If you could have any single tabloid story actually come true, which one would it be?

If you could give a single piece of advice to the fashion industry right now, what would you say?

If you were on the committee to assign ratings to films, how would you define the categories?

—◁◆▷—

If you could have any single option added to your automobile, what would it be?

—◁◆▷—

If you could have one new store added to your local mall, what would it be?

If you could have prevented the bombing of any single city during a war in this century, which would it be?

If you could have participated in any march on Washington, which would you have been part of?

If you had known one thing that you didn't when you had your first sexual experience, what would it be?

If you had to name the one thing you did as a child to most torment your sibling(s), what was it that you did?

67

If you could have a lifetime 50 percent discount in any single store at your local mall, which store would it be in?

If you were to have a weekend of sex with a person you would normally consider to be "beneath" you, who would you pick?

If you were to pick the one child you know who you would predict to be the most successful in life, who would it be?

If you could have been present at any one ticker-tape parade, which would you choose?

If you could have a copy of *The New York Times* from any single day in history, which would it be?

If you were Madonna, what would you do for your next publicity stunt?

⊢⊶ ⊫⬧☰ ⊷⊣

If you could be given the complete film library of the work of a single actor, who would you pick?

⊢⊶ ⊫⬧☰ ⊷⊣

If you could retract one expression of gratitude that you made erroneously, what would you take back?

If you could tell your mother or father one thing that you haven't, what would it be?

If you were invited to the White House for dinner tonight, what would you wear from your current wardrobe?

—·—≡·≡—·—

If you had to name one person who should not have divorced their spouse, who would you pick?

—·—≡·≡—·—

If you were to become a prostitute, how much money do you think you could charge per hour?

If you had to choose the hour of day when time goes slowest, what would you say?

＋· ⅍◈⅀ ·＋

If you could have your spouse say one thing about you to friends, what would you want him or her to say?

＋· ⅍◈⅀ ·＋

If you had to guess the one thing your mate says about you to friends, what would you say it is?

＋· ⅍◈⅀ ·＋

If you had to identify the most extreme example of ingratitude you can think of from your own experiences, what would it be?

If you could freeze your mate's looks at one age, but you would grow older, what age would you pick?

----- ◄◆► -----

If you had to name the worst thing you've ever done to someone emotionally, what would it be?

----- ◄◆► -----

If you spoke English with a certain type of American accent other than your own, what would you want it to be?

----- ◄◆► -----

If you spoke English with a foreign accent, which would you want it to be?

72

If you had to name a song whose lyrics best captured an experience you had, which would it be?

If, from all the people you know, you were to pick a person whose name truly suits them, who would you choose?

If you could take back one gift you have given, but now wish you hadn't, what would it be?

If you could guarantee the happiness of any single person in the world because they most deserve it, who would it be?

If you had to choose the most beautiful name of an existing country, what would you choose?

If you could make someone you know less ignorant about one thing, who would you pick, and what would it be?

If every night you could have one singer appear to serenade you, who would you choose?

If you could learn the total number of hours you have spent in your life doing one thing, what would it be?

If you had to name the person you know with the best attitude regarding money, who would it be?

If you could have only one magazine subscription for life, which would you pick?

If you had to name the biggest hypocrite you have ever met, who would win?

If you could repeat one experience you had with your mate, what would it be?

75

If you could get a massage every day from one person, from whom would you want it to be?

—— ≡◆≡ ——

If you could dedicate a song on the radio right now to your lover or spouse, which song would you pick?

—— ≡◆≡ ——

If you had to nominate the worst-dressed person you know, who would it be?

If you had to choose the most necessary thing you do each day, what would you say it was?

If you could pair up any two single people you know, who would you pick?

—·— ⊠✦⊠ —·—

If you were to decide on a new punishment for convicted murderers, aside from life imprisonment or the death penalty, what would it be?

—·— ⊠✦⊠ —·—

If you could have your mate surprise you by doing one thing (other than give you a gift), what would you want them to do?

—·— ⊠✦⊠ —·—

If you could fall asleep each night with your head resting upon anything other than your pillow, what would it be?

If you could choose someone you know to be a guest on a television show, who would it be, and on which show?

If you were to guess which of all the people you know platonically is the best in bed, who would you pick?

If you had to rely on one person you know in any difficult situation, who would you pick?

If you had to work in any store at your local mall, which would it be?

If you could have one extra hour each day to do only one thing, what would you do in that hour?

If you had a bust of yourself sculpted, where would you place it?

If you had been Marcia Clark, what one thing would you have done differently in the O. J. Simpson trial?

If your birthday could be in a different month of the year, when would you have it?

If you were to describe an act of true loyalty that you have witnessed, what would it be, and who performed it?

If you could arrange for one thing to happen to your spouse, without them knowing you arranged it, what would you plan?

If you could gain proof of someone's guilt about something, what would it be?

If you could destroy one thing physically, what would it be, and how would you do it?

If the laziest person you know had to do one thing each day for the rest of their life, who would it be, and what would they have to do?

If you could teach one person you know a lesson about money, who would it be, and what would they learn?

If you could be more focused in one area of your life, what would it be?

If you were to pick the most amoral person you know and teach them a single lesson, who and what would it be?

If you could rename every person in your family, what would they each be called?

If you could have the lips of any living person, whose would you want?

If you could avoid any one physical ailment in your old age, what would it be?

If you could throw a great Halloween party anywhere, where would you have it?

If you had to name the best example of fate that you know, what would you say?

+———— ⊯✦⊯ ————+

If you could touch only one part of your own body for the rest of your life, where would you choose to touch?

If you had to name the book from your childhood that had the biggest influence on you, what book would it be?

+———— ⊯✦⊯ ————+

If you could punish the most difficult person you work with on a daily basis, what would you do, and to whom?

83

If you could have your license plate say anything at all, what would it be?

⚏

If you had to pick the most beautiful word in your own language, what would you choose?

⚏

If you had to describe yourself as a child in one word, what would it be?

⚏

If you had to name a single song or album that you most associate with a particular period of your life, what song would you choose, and from what year?

84

If you had to describe the moment in your life when you had to have the most courage, what would you say?

If you could avoid ever having to see a certain relative again, who would it be?

    ＋ ≡◆≡ ＋

If you were to describe true generosity by using an example you witnessed, what would you use?

    ＋ ≡◆≡ ＋

If you had to recount your worst case of putting your foot in your mouth, when was it?

If you could go back and express gratitude about one thing in your life, for what would it be, and to whom?

If you were to give an award to someone for being the most moral person, who would win, and what would the award be?

If you were to name the person or people you have the most compassion for, who would it be?

If you could ask your best friend one question you have never had the nerve to ask, what would it be?

If you could have kept a detailed diary of one period of your life, so that you could now reread it, what period would it be from?

+—+ ≡♦≡ +—+

If you had to name the one situation that would overwhelm your courage, what would it be?

+—+ ≡♦≡ +—+

If you were to describe your first kiss, what would you say?

+—+ ≡♦≡ +—+

If you devoted the next year to making as much money as possible above all else, how would you do it?

87

If you had to name the most difficult thing about being a teenager today, what would you say?

If you could change one thing about your love life, what would it be?

If you had to name the most embarrassing moment of your life, when was it?

If you could be given a personal tour of any Hollywood celebrity's house, whose would you want to see?

If you had to name the one thing you worried about most in high school, what was it, and did it merit all the fuss?

If you could make one change to your favorite mall, what would it be?

If you could modify your computer in any single way, how would you make it be different?

If you could find the personal diary of one person from history, with all the juicy details, whose would you want to find?

89

If you could define the legal limitations for pornography, what would you propose?

If you were to name the one possession that means the most to you, what would it be?

If you had to name a person who was the most important role model in your life, who would it be?

If the United States had to sacrifice one state, which one would you give away?

If you could communicate with any type of animal, which would you pick?

If you could have the sense of humor of anyone you know, whose would it be?

＋ ≍✦≍ ＋

If you had to name a time when you helped a stranger the most, when was it?

＋ ≍✦≍ ＋

If you had to recall the nicest compliment ever given to you, what would it be?

91

If you had to name the most difficult period of your life, when would it be?

—+— ≍◆≍ —+—

If you could have a stranger come up to you and whisper anything into your ear, what would you want them to say?

—+— ≍◆≍ —+—

If you could give one piece of advice to the Republican party, what would it be?

—+— ≍◆≍ —+—

If you could implement a strategy to fight the war on drugs, what would it entail?

If you were to decide what legal rights gays and lesbians should have with regard to marriage and children, what would they be?

If you had to describe your most recurring dream, what would it be?

If you had to pick one of your personality traits as being the best, which would it be?

If you could havet one more pet, what kind would you get, and what would you name it?

If you had the gift of magic for one day, what would you do?

If you had to name the one thing that has changed the most about growing up since your childhood, what would it be?

If you could pump enormous amounts of money into one area of scientific research, what would it be for?

If you could force someone very rich to give away all their money for a single cause, who would you pick, and what cause would it go to?

If a one-year period of your diary were to be published, what year would you want it to be?

If you could have one person you have lost touch with call you up tonight and invite you to dinner, who would you want it to be?

If you had to name the one area of your life that you are the least self-disciplined in, what would it be?

If you could decide exactly how, when, and where your children would learn sex education, what would you consider to be ideal?

If you had to describe the perfect retirement home, what would it be like?

If you had to name the subject you took in school that turned out to be least useful or worthwhile, what would it be?

⊷ ⧓ ⊶

If you could give one piece of advice to the Democratic party, what would it be?

⊷ ⧓ ⊶

If you were asked to define what a feminist is in one sentence, what would your response be?

96

If you could be sainted for doing one thing in life, what would it be for?

If you could change one thing about your marriage, what would you alter?

If you could establish criteria for the right to be a parent, what would they be?

If you could enact one law that applied only to your own family, what would it be?

97

If you could revise the current parole laws, what would you want to do?

If you could have named the first woman something other than Eve, what name would you pick?

If you could have named the first man something other than Adam, what would you pick?

If you could own a single prop from any film ever made, what would you choose?

If you could have done one thing with one of your teachers, what would it be, and with whom?

If you could retrieve one toy or stuffed animal from your childhood, which one would you recover?

If you could wake up tomorrow in your own bed next to anyone or anything, who or what would it be?

If you could do one thing to revise the welfare system, what would you do?

If you had to name a person you know who would be the easiest to seduce, who would it be?

If you were to have the voice of one media personality, whose would it be?

‹‹‹ ≍◊≍ ›››

If you could have God perform one miracle today, what would you wish it to be?

‹‹‹ ≍◊≍ ›››

If you could regulate (or deregulate) smoking, what rules would you make (or repeal)?

100

If you could receive more affection from someone you know from now on, who would you want it to be from?

—+— ⚜ —+—

If you could look through anyone's personnel file at work, whose would you pick?

—+— ⚜ —+—

If you had to recall the one time in your childhood or adolescence when you made your parents the most angry, when was it?

—+— ⚜ —+—

If you could reform the health care system right now, how would you do it?

101

If you had to name the one thing you have done that most pleased your parents, what would you say?

If you had to name the person who most objected to your choice of mate, who would it be?

If you could do one thing right now that isn't being done to help solve the problem of AIDS, what would it be?

If you could own one article of clothing from any film ever made, what would you take?

If you were to sleep with any famous couple, who would you choose?

              ——— ≡◊≡ ———

If you had to name the issue that will be the most important in the next election, what would you say?

              ——— ≡◊≡ ———

If you could have studied one subject in school that you didn't, or that wasn't offered, what would it be?

              ——— ≡◊≡ ———

If you had to have one job that you have had previously, which one would you want again?

If you were to name the greatest sexual advantage that women have over men, what would it be?

If your community decided to build low-cost housing, where would you propose it be located?

If you could have the autograph of any athlete you do not have, whose would it be, and what would you like them to sign?

If you could set the guidelines for gun control, what would they be?

If you were given the power to settle the issue of gays in the military, what policy would you set?

If you had to name the best sexual advantage that men have over women, what would it be?

If you could have the original baseball card of any three players in history, who would they be?

If you could relive any single family outing in your life, what would it be?

If you had to pick one foreign language that students would be required to learn in school, what would it be?

If you could set the national speed limit for all highways, what would it be?

If you could sit and have a beer with three sports figures from any time, who would you pick?

If you could be emotionally closer to one member of your family, who would it be?

If you had to pick the member of your family who is least like the others, who would it be?

If you had to pick the worst teacher from your childhood, who would win the prize?

If you were to describe your favorite sexual fantasy, what would it be?

If you were in charge of the military budget, what is the first thing you would do?

107

If you had to choose the person from your family you most admire, who would it be?

———❧———

If you were six inches tall for a day, what would you do?

———❧———

If you could have anyone in the world stop by for a visit, who would you want it to be?

If the world were to turn to one single source of energy tomorrow, what would you want it to be?

If you had to pick the teacher you've had who would be the most disappointed with how your life turned out, who would it be?

If you had to name the world's most pressing environmental concern, what would it be?

If you had to pick the most embarrassing thing your parents did to you as a child, what was it?

If you could have one television sitcom set as your real home, which show would it be from?

109

If you were to have someone's autograph tattooed somewhere on your body, whose would it be, and where would you put it?

If you could rename any sports team, which would you pick, and what would you rename it?

If you could add one required course to the present school system, what would it be?

If you could revise the income tax system, what would you propose?

If you could have the personality of any TV character, whose would you adopt?

If you could pass one law to help the environment, what would it be?

        —◦—◄◆►—◦—

If you could retake one course you took in high school or college, which would it be?

        —◦—◄◆►—◦—

If you could make one change to your garden, what would it be?

If you were to set your country's immigration policy, what would it be?

If you were to describe the worst poverty you have ever seen, what would you say?

If you could grow the world's most perfect specimen of plant or flower, what would it be?

If you could impose a heavy luxury tax on any single item, what would it be?

If you could go back to high school to relive one event exactly as it happened, what would you pick?

⚬—⚬ ☰◆☰ ⚬—⚬

If you could go back to high school to relive one event as you wish it had been, what would it be?

⚬—⚬ ☰◆☰ ⚬—⚬

If you were to name the most ridiculous lawsuit you have ever heard about, what would it be?

⚬—⚬ ☰◆☰ ⚬—⚬

If you were to select the person you know who would be the most difficult to seduce, who would you name?

If you could spend next New Year's Eve doing anything, what would you do, and with whom?

—◆—

If you could have been present during the inauguration of any past president, whose would it be?

—◆—

If you could un-tax anything now currently taxed, what would you pick?

—◆—

If you could have season tickets for any team, sitting in any place in the stadium, which team would it be and where would you sit?

114

If you were to spend a week anywhere alone without contact with civilization, where would you go?

If you could ski in any place in the world, where would you go?

＊＋＝＋＝＋＊

If you had to choose a television personality to be president of the United States, who would you pick?

＊＋＝＋＝＋＊

If you could be caressed by the hands of any person you have known platonically, whose would they be?

If you had to name the person you know with the sexiest phone voice, who would win?

⊶ ⋈ ⊷

If you could relocate your entire workplace to a new location, where would you want it to be?

If you were to be the first lady (or first man), what would you want your role to be?

⊶ ⋈ ⊷

If you had to be stuck for hours in any airport, which would you want it to be in?

If you could spend an entire day in any zoo by yourself, which zoo would you pick to be in, and what would you do?

 ⸻

If you could have an entire city depopulated to explore with a friend for one week, what city would it be, and what would you do?

 ⸻

If you had to recall your worst travel experience, what would it be?

 ⸻

If you had to give up one of your vices for Lent next year, which would you sacrifice?

117

If you could make one person jealous, who would it be, and how would you do it?

If you had to guess that two people at work were having an affair, who would you pair?

If you did not work, how much TV would you watch every day?

If you had to pick the TV personality you were most in love with as a kid, who would it be?

If you were to make any hotel room your home for a year, where would it be?

If you could live in a past era just so you could wear the clothes in fashion at the time, when would it be?

If you could redesign the uniforms of any sports team, which team would it be, and what changes would you make?

If you could kiss anyone in the world on one spot other than the lips, who would you choose, and where would you kiss them?

119

If you had to name the best speech given at the Academy Awards, whose was it?

If God were to appear before you in any form, what form would you want Him to take?

If you were to give anyone a raise at work (other than yourself), who would you give it to?

If you had to name the hardest position to play in sports, what would you say it is?

If you could frame the jockstrap of any sports figure and hang it in your den, whose would you choose?

If you had to describe the thing done by someone at work that drives you the craziest, what would you say?

If you had to name the next person who should be fired at your place of employment, who would you choose?

If you were to name one person you know who is a true gentleman, who would it be?

If you were to define the word *courage* by giving an example, how would you do it?

⸻

If you had to pick the one institution you have the most faith in, what would you say?

⸻

If you were to be the opposite sex for a single day, what would you do?

⸻

If you could play a prank on anyone at work with impunity, what would you do, and to whom?

122

If you could go back to one place you have been in your life, where would you go?

If you had to be addicted to one thing, what would it be?

If you were to have the hands of someone you know, whose would you want?

If you could remove the ability to hate from one person in the world today, who would it be?

If you could be any sign of the zodiac other than your own, what would you want to be?

<hr>

If you could run any existing charity, which would it be?

If you could insist that one person you work with deliver coffee to you every day, who would you chose?

<hr>

If you could have taken part in any single historical ceremony, what would it have been?

If you were to name the one choice in life that you would never want to make again, what would it be?

If you had to disguise yourself physically, how would you do it?

If you could have one science fiction story come true, which would it be?

If you had to have the hair of a current politician, whose would you pick?

If you could remove one marking from your skin, which one would it be?

⊰ ⊱

If you had to choose, from among your current friends, one person to be your partner in a new business venture, who would you choose?

⊰ ⊱

If you were to name the most obnoxious tourists you've encountered, who would they be?

⊰ ⊱

If you had to eliminate forever one form of weather, what would it be?

126

If you could go back to an incident in your past, in order to act more honorably than you did, what situation would it be?

If you could gain back all the hours you've spent in your life doing a certain thing, what would it be?

If you could have one piece of jewelry belonging to someone you know personally, what would you pick?

If you could ensure one thing about Heaven besides its existence, what would it be?

127

If you were to get a divorce, what is the one thing you would fight for above all else (besides your children)?

—————◄◆►—————

If you could have had any job in history, what would it have been?

—————◄◆►—————

If you could ensure that one existing law would never be broken by anyone, which would it be?

—————◄◆►—————

If you could go back in time to undo one injury you inflicted on someone else, what would it be?

128

If you had to name the one person you have been most jealous of, who would win?

If you had to name the one thing about your life right now that you would not change, what would it be?

If you could receive a kiss from anyone in the world on one part of your body other than your lips, who would you want to kiss you, and where?

If you could forget one thing, what would it be?

If you have an interesting or humorous question or answer to contribute to sequels of *If . . .*, we would love to hear from you. Please send your response or new question to the address below. Please give us your name and age, and sign and date your contribution. Thank you.

Evelyn McFarlane
James Saywell
c/o Villard Books
201 East 50th Street
New York, NY 10022

About the Authors

Evelyn McFarlane was born in Brooklyn and grew up in San Diego. She received her degree in architecture from Cornell University and has worked in New York and Boston. She is now living in an Umbrian hill town in Italy and spends her time painting, writing, and teaching.

She dedicates this sequel to Adam Drisin for his support and unfaltering belief in the book.

James Saywell was born in Canada. He studied architecture in Toronto and Princeton. He divides his time between designing buildings and furniture, painting, writing, and teaching architecture, and between the United States and Italy. This is his second book.

He dedicates this book to his parents, who taught him the importance of questioning.